MW00651333

CogAT® Screening Form
Practice Test
GRADE 3
LEVEL 9

Practice Questions from the CogAT® Form 7 / 8 Analogies Sections: Verbal/Picture Analogies, Number Analogies, & Figure Matrices.

ISBN: 978-1-948255-88-2

The Cognitive Abilities Test (CogAT®) is a registered trademark of Houghton Mifflin Harcourt, which is not affiliated with Origins Publications. Houghton Mifflin Harcourt has not endorsed the contents of this book.

Origins Publications
New York, NY, USA

Email:info@originspublications.com

BONUS

DOWNLOAD QUANTITATIVE CHALLENGE QUESTIONS

If you also want additional quantitative challenge questions, please go to the following link to download them!

To get your challenge questions today, please visit:
https://originstutoring.lpages.co/cogat3analogiesquestions/

Challenge questions can help a student get used to doing the most difficult questions on the test.

Get the questions now at
https://originstutoring.lpages.co/cogat3analogiesquestions/

Origins Publications

Origins Publications helps students develop their higher-order thinking skills while also improving their chances of admission into gifted and accelerated-learner programs.

Our goal is to unleash and nurture the genius in every student. We do this by offering educational and test prep materials that are fun, challenging and provide a sense of accomplishment.

Please contact us with any questions.

info@originspublications.com

Contents

Part 1: Introduction to the CogAT® Screening Form

This book offers an overview of the types of questions on the CogAT® Level 9 Screening Form, test-taking strategies to improve performance, sample questions, and a full-length practice CogAT Screening Form practice test that students can use to assess their knowledge and practice their test-taking skills. It is important that you read this entire introduction!

Who Takes this Test?

The CogAT Level 9 Screening Form is a test that is often used as an expedient yet reliable assessment tool or admissions test in 3rd grade for entry into gifted and talented (GATE) programs and highly-competitive schools.

What is the Difference Between the CogAT® and the CogAT® Screening Form?

The CogAT Screening Form is a shorter version of the full length CogAT Form 7. The Screening Form contains only the analogies section of each battery: picture/verbal analogies, number analogies, and figure matrices.

Some schools prefer the CogAT Screening Form, as the test offers a quality evaluation with a shorter administration time than the complete CogAT.

When Does the CogAT® Screening Form Test Take Place?

This depends on the school district you reside in or want to attend. Check with the relevant school/district to learn more about test dates and the application/ registration process.

CogAT® Level 9 Screening Form Overview

The CogAT Screening Form is a group-administered test that features only the analogies section of each of the three independent 'batteries': Verbal, Quantitative, and Nonverbal. It is designed to assess learned reasoning in these three areas, which experts believe are the areas most closely linked to academic achievement.

The CogAT Screening Form covers topics that students may not see in school, so kids will need to think a little differently in order to do well.

Length

Students take about 30 minutes to complete the test.

Format

The test is made up of 60 multiple choice questions.

Test Sections

Verbal Analogies: Students are provided with two words that form a pair, as well as a third word. From the answer choices, the student must select the word that goes with the third provided word.

Figure Matrices: Students are given a 2x2 matrix with the image missing in one cell. Students must determine the relationship between the two spatial forms in the top row and find a fourth image that has the same relationship to the spatial form in the bottom row.

Number Analogies: Students are provided with two sets of analogous numbers, and a third set with a missing number. To determine the missing number, students must find the relationship between the numbers in each of the first two sets, and apply it to the final set.

Part 2: How to Use this Book

The CogAT Screening Form is an important test and the more a student is familiar with the questions on the exam, the better she will fare when taking the test.

This book will help your student get used to the format and content of the test so s/he will be adequately prepared and feel confident on test day.

Inside this book, you will find:

- Sample question for each question type on the test and teaching tips to help your student approach each question type strategically and with confidence.

- CogAT® Level 9 Screening Form practice test.

- Access to bonus 'CHALLENGE' CogAT analogies questions. See end page of this book for more information.

Part 3. Test Prep Tips and Strategies

Firstly, and most importantly, commit to make the test preparation process a stress-free one. A student's ability to keep calm and focused in the face of challenge is a quality that will benefit her throughout her academic life.

Be prepared for difficult questions from the get-go! There will be a certain percentage of questions that are very challenging for all children (or all ages for that matter!). It is key to encourage students to use all strategies available when faced with challenging questions. And remember that a student can get quite a few questions wrong and still do very well on the test.

Before starting the practice test, go through the sample questions and read the teaching tips provided at the beginning of the book. They will help you guide your student as he or she progresses through the practice test.

The following strategies may also be useful as you help your student prepare:

Before You Start

Find a quiet, comfortable spot to work free of distractions. Show your student how to perform the simple technique of shading (and erasing) bubbles.

During Prep

If your student is challenged by a question, ask your student to explain why he or she chose a specific answer. If the answer was incorrect, this will help you identify where your student is stumbling. If the answer was correct, asking your student to articulate her reasoning aloud will help reinforce the concept.

Encourage your student to carefully consider all the answer options before selecting one. Tell him or her there is only ONE answer.

If your student is stumped by a question, she or he can use the process of elimination. First, encourage your student to eliminate obviously wrong answers to narrow down the answer choices. If your student is still in doubt after using this technique, tell him or her to guess as there are no points deducted for wrong answers.

Review all the questions your student answered incorrectly, and explain to your student why the answer is incorrect. Have your student attempt these questions again a few days later to see if he now understands the concept.

Encourage your student to do her best, but take plenty of study breaks. Start with 10-15 minute sessions. Your student will perform best if she views these activities as fun and engaging, not as exercises to be avoided.

Verbal Analogies Sample Question and Tips

There are 22 Verbal Analogies questions in the CogAT® Level 9 Screening Form.

SAMPLE QUESTION:

Find the relationship between the first two words, then choose a word that has the same relationship with the third word.

teacher : student   as   doctor :

A. hospital   B. patient   C. passenger   D. medicine   E. customer

Correct Answer: **B.** A teacher helps students as a doctor helps patients.

TEACHING TIPS

- To master analogies, a student needs to have general background knowledge, and an understanding/recognition of various relationships, including:

  → Object/function — One word in a pair describes the purpose or function of the other word.

  → Agent (person or animal)/location.

  → Agent (person or animal)/action.

  → Definition/Evidence—One word in a pair helps to define the other word; or, one word in a pair is a defining characteristic of the other word.

  → Synonym/Antonym—One word in a pair is a synonym or antonym of the other word.

  → Degree/Intensity—Both words in a pair are similar in concept, but vary in intensity.

  → Component/Part—One word in a pair represents one part of the other word, which represents a whole; or, one word is simply a component of the other.

- As often as possible, incorporate discussions about similarities, differences, and relationships between words into your everyday conversation with your student. Help your student begin thinking about how different words and concepts are connected to one another.

- When answering practice questions, teach your student to determine the relationship between the first pair of words before looking at the answer choices. Once your student determines the relationship between the first pair, she can then look at the answer choices to find the pair with the exact same relationship.

Figure Matrices Sample Question and Tips

There are 20 Figure Matrices questions in the CogAT® Level 9 Screening Form.

SAMPLE QUESTION:

Look at the shapes in the boxes on top. These shapes go together in a certain way. Which answer choice belongs where the question mark is?

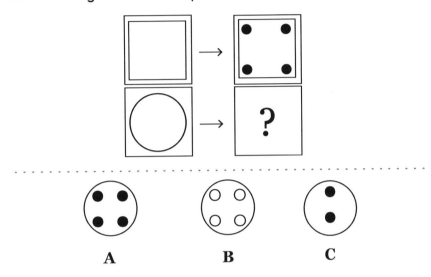

Correct Answer: **A.** In the top row, there are two figures that go together in a certain way. They go together in the sense that as the figure moves from left box to right box, it stays the same shape (a square) but adds four black circles inside.

Your student needs to find the figure among the answer options that fits best in the question mark box on the bottom row. The correct choice will have the same relationship with the figure on the bottom row that the figures in the top row have with each other.

Option B is incorrect because, although the figure is the same shape as the figure on the bottom row, the inside circles that are added are white. Option C is incorrect because, although the figure is the same shape as the figure on the bottom row, only two black inside circles are added. Option A is correct as the figure has the same shape (circle) as the figure on the bottom row and it has four black circles inside.

- Make sure your student knows key concepts that come up in these types of questions, including geometric concepts such as rotational symmetry, line symmetry, parts of a whole.

- If your student is finding these items difficult, encourage her to discover the pattern by isolating one element (e.g: outer shape, inner shape/s) and identify how it changes:

  → Ask: Is the color/shading of the element changing as it moves?

  → Ask: Is the element changing positions as it moves? Does it move up or down? Clockwise or counter-clockwise? Does it end up in the opposite (mirror) position?

  → Ask: Does the element disappear or increase in number as it moves along the row? Does it get bigger or smaller?

- Encourage your student to make a prediction for the missing object and compare the description with the answer choices.

Number Analogies Sample Question and Tips

There are 18 Number Analogies questions in the CogAT® Level 9 Screening Form.

SAMPLE QUESTION: Find the relationship between the numbers in the first set, and between the numbers in the second set. Then choose a number which follows the same pattern when paired with the number in the third set.

[10   →   2]   [20   →   4]   [30   →   ?]

    A. 3   B. 5   C. 6   D. 4   E. 10

Correct Answer: C. The rule is to divide the first number in each set by 5, so the answer is 6 (option C).

TEACHING TIPS

- Your student is probably not accustomed to completing number matrices, so it is important to frequently expose him to this question type in order to build confidence and familiarity.

- Show how to approach solving a number matrix by "thinking aloud" as you work through a question with your student.

- Work with your student on basic mathematical concepts, including addition, subtraction, division, multiplication.

COGAT® SCREENING FORM
PRACTICE TEST

VERBAL BATTERY

• •

VERBAL ANALOGIES

• •

For each item, the student is presented with two words that have a relationship or go together in a particular way.

The student needs to figure out the relationship between the first two words. The student then needs to choose the word in the answer choices that has the same relationship with the third word.

VERBAL ANALOGIES

1. **candle : wax as window : ?**

    A. door   **B.** fabric   **C.** open   **D.** glass   **E.** plastic

2. **dog : mammal as frog : ?**

    A. slimy   **B.** amphibian   **C.** reptile   **D.** animal   **E.** toad

3. **football : field as tennis : ?**

    A. sport   **B.** track   **C.** ring   **D.** court   **E.** ball

4. **cotton : fabric as gold : ?**

    A. scarf   **B.** metal   **C.** umbrella   **D.** saucepan   **E.** wool

5. **desert : sand as lake : ?**

    A. blue   **B.** fish   **C.** cactus   **D.** boat   **E.** water

VERBAL ANALOGIES

6. **rowboat : oar as car : ?**

   A. door   **B.** road   **C.** drive   **D.** truck   **E.** steering wheel

7. **spots : ladybug as stripes : ?**

   A. leopard   **B.** tiger   **C.** elephant   **D.** stars   **E.** ant

8. **rein : rain as there : ?**

   A. them   **B.** rare   **C.** their   **D.** are   **E.** that

9. **clock : time as ruler : ?**

   A. distance   **B.** measure   **C.** inches   **D.** volume   **E.** numbers

10. **teacher : student as doctor : ?**

    A. hospital   **B.** patient   **C.** passenger   **D.** medicine   **E.** customer

11. **three : triangle as eight : ?**

    A. square   **B.** shape   **C.** octagon   **D.** circle   **E.** pentagon

12. **pear : pair as hare : ?**

    A. rabbit   **B.** shoes   **C.** hair   **D.** hairy   **E.** hares

13. **nail polish : nails as earring : ?**

    A. diamond   **B.** beauty   **C.** ears   **D.** jewelry   **E.** lips

14. **I am : I'm as you are : ?**

    A. you're   **B.** yours   **C.** you'd   **D.** you   **E.** are

15. **bee : larva as fly : ?**

    A. baby   **B.** chrysalis   **C.** insect   **D.** tadpole   **E.** maggot

VERBAL ANALOGIES

16. **spider : web as wasp : ?**

   A. sting   **B.** hive   **C.** nest   **D.** pit   **E.** den

17. **amusing : hilarious as sad : ?**

   A. giggle   **B.** unacceptable   **C.** devastating   **D.** happy   **E.** hurt

18. **ring : finger as tie : ?**

   A. body   **B.** neck   **C.** suit   **D.** clothing   **E.** jewelry

19. **swift : leopard as slow : ?**

   A. rapid   **B.** lion   **C.** horse   **D.** snail   **E.** walk

20. **comb: hair as hammer: ?**

   A. nail   **B.** brush   **C.** tool   **D.** workshed   **E.** screwdriver

21. **white : black as before : ?**

    A. over   **B.** color   **C.** advance   **D.** gray   **E.** after

22. **mansion : shack as yacht : ?**

    A. paddle   **B.** ocean   **C.** sail   **D.** dinghy   **E.** mobile

NONVERBAL BATTERY

• • • • • • • • • • • • •

FIGURE MATRICES

• • • • • • • • • • • • • • • • • •

Figure Matrices

Look at the shapes in the boxes on top. These shapes go together in a certain way. Which shape belongs where the question mark is?

1

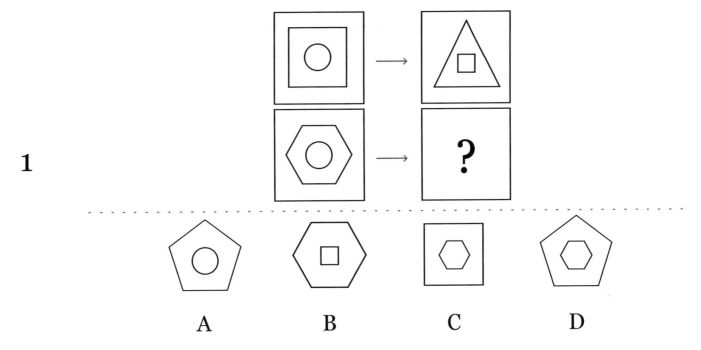

| A | B | C | D |

Look at the shapes in the boxes on top. These shapes go together in a certain way. Which shape belongs where the question mark is?

2

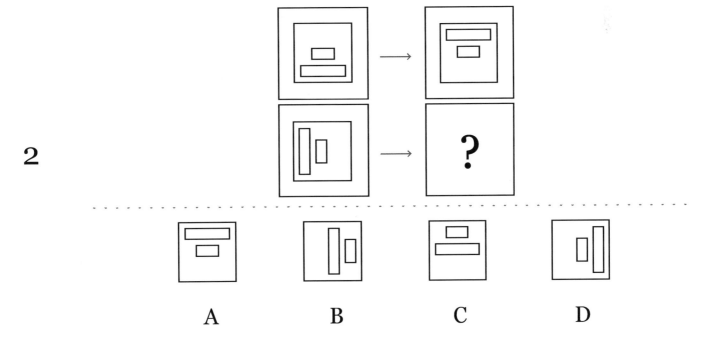

| A | B | C | D |

Figure Matrices

Look at the shapes in the boxes on top. These shapes go together in a certain way. Which shape belongs where the question mark is?

3

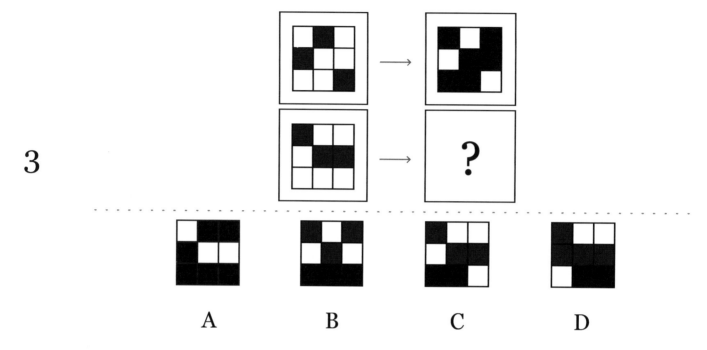

| A | B | C | D |

Look at the shapes in the boxes on top. These shapes go together in a certain way. Which shape belongs where the question mark is?

4

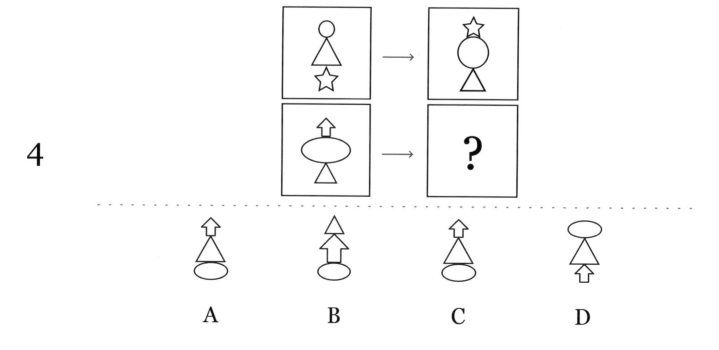

| A | B | C | D |

CogAT Screening Form Test Prep Book

Figure Matrices

Look at the shapes in the boxes on top. These shapes go together in a certain way. Which shape belongs where the question mark is?

5

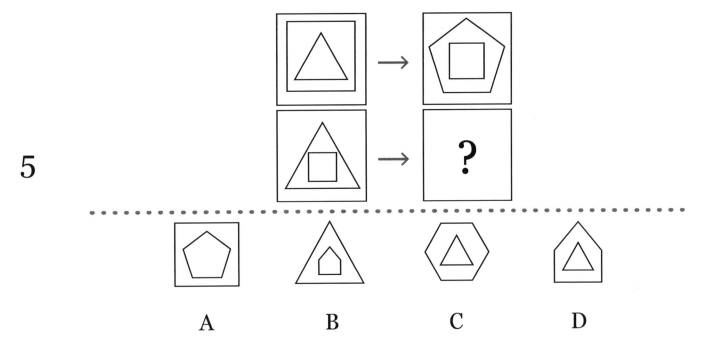

A   B   C   D

Look at the shapes in the boxes on top. These shapes go together in a certain way. Which shape belongs where the question mark is?

6

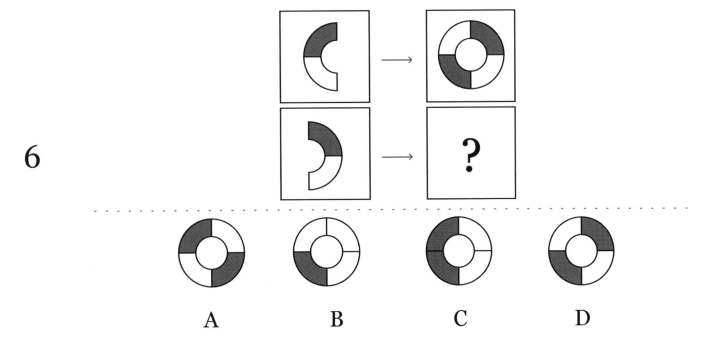

A   B   C   D

Figure Matrices

Look at the shapes in the boxes on top. These shapes go together in a certain way. Which shape belongs where the question mark is?

7

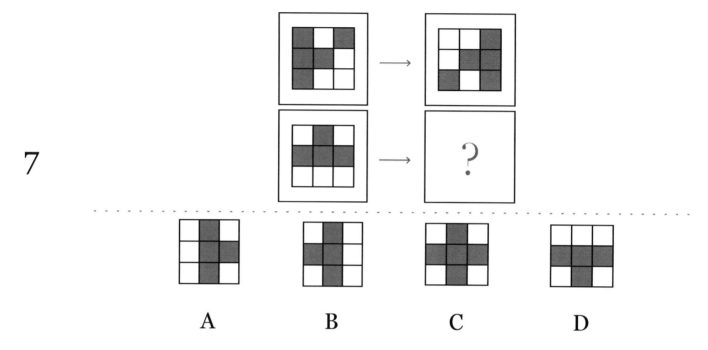

A   B   C   D

Look at the shapes in the boxes on top. These shapes go together in a certain way. Which shape belongs where the question mark is?

8

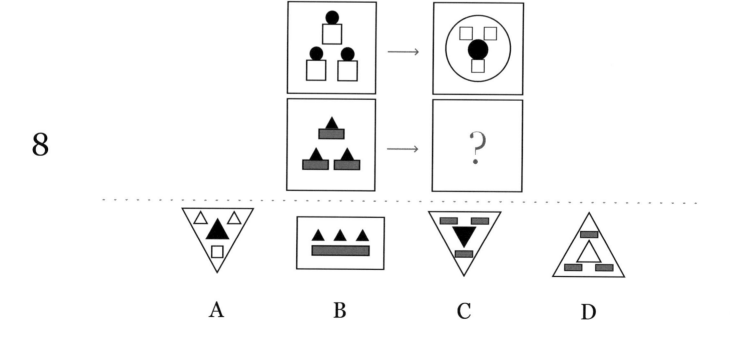

A   B   C   D

Figure Matrices

Look at the shapes in the boxes on top. These shapes go together in a certain way.
Which shape belongs where the question mark is?

9

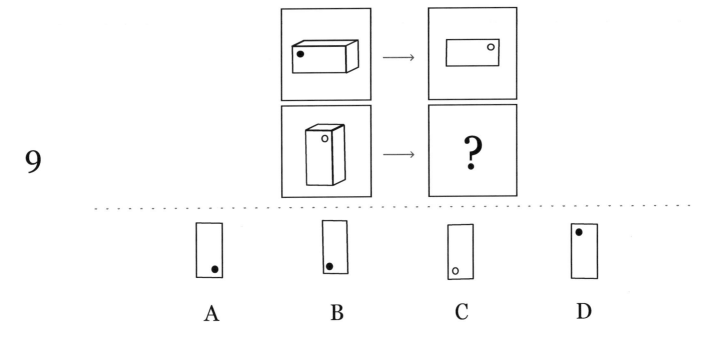

A   B   C   D

Look at the shapes in the boxes on top. These shapes go together in a certain way.
Which shape belongs where the question mark is?

10

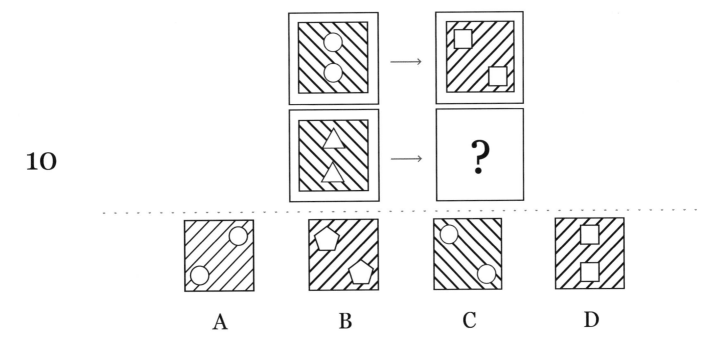

A   B   C   D

Figure Matrices

Look at the shapes in the boxes on top. These shapes go together in a certain way. Which shape belongs where the question mark is?

11

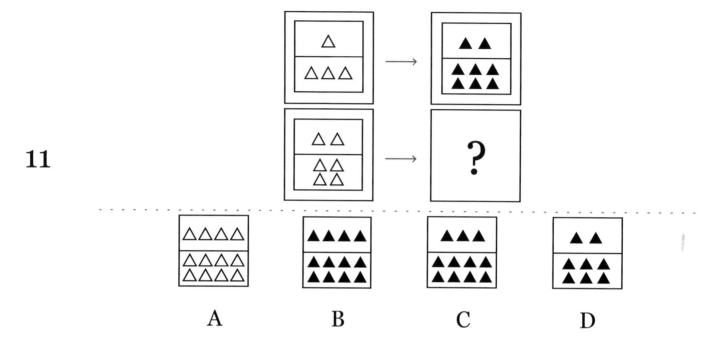

A   B   C   D

Look at the shapes in the boxes on top. These shapes go together in a certain way. Which shape belongs where the question mark is?

12

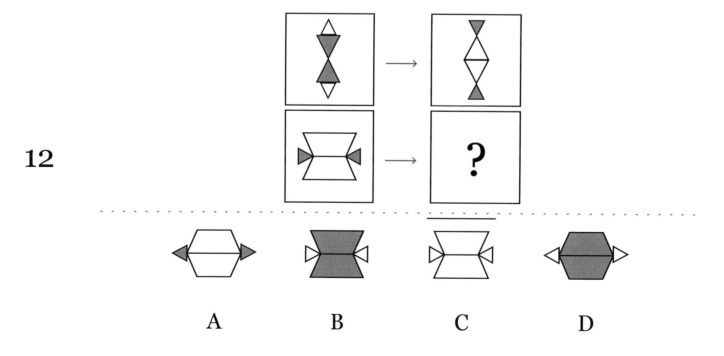

A   B   C   D

Figure Matrices

Look at the shapes in the boxes on top. These shapes go together in a certain way. Which shape belongs where the question mark is?

13

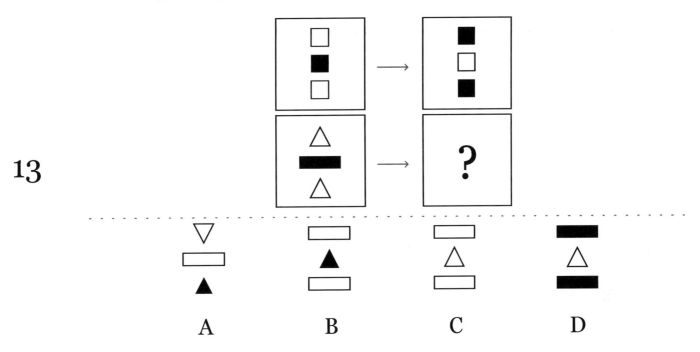

Look at the shapes in the boxes on top. These shapes go together in a certain way. Which shape belongs where the question mark is?

14

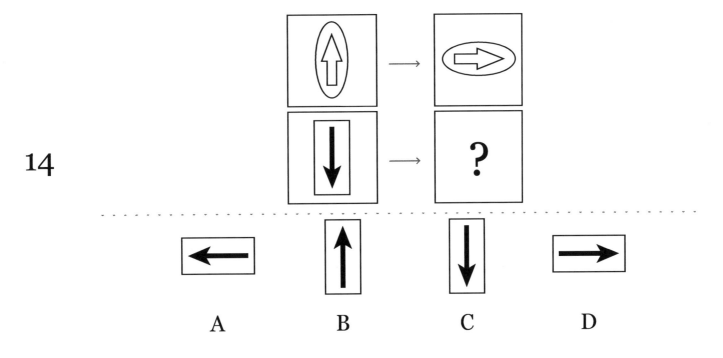

Figure Matrices

Look at the shapes in the boxes on top. These shapes go together in a certain way. Which shape belongs where the question mark is?

15

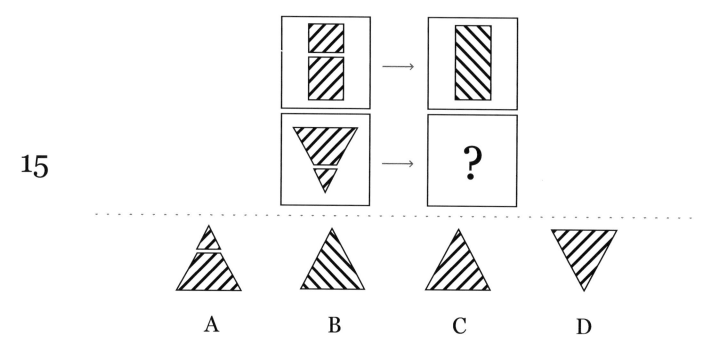

A   B   C   D

Look at the shapes in the boxes on top. These shapes go together in a certain way. Which shape belongs where the question mark is?

16

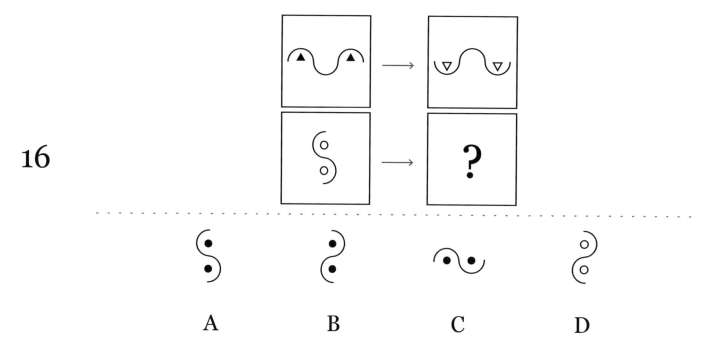

A   B   C   D

Figure Matrices

Look at the shapes in the boxes on top. These shapes go together in a certain way. Which shape belongs where the question mark is?

17

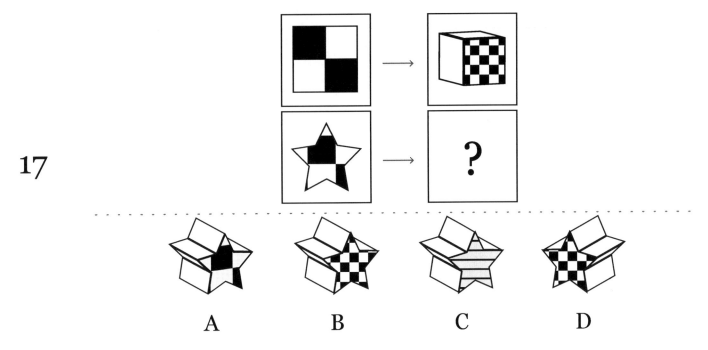

Look at the shapes in the boxes on top. These shapes go together in a certain way. Which shape belongs where the question mark is?

18

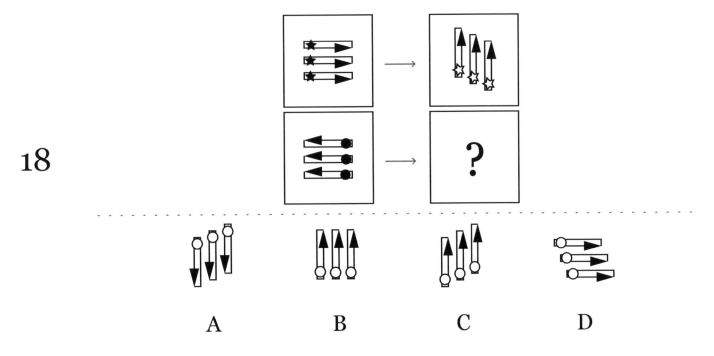

Figure Matrices

Look at the shapes in the boxes on top. These shapes go together in a certain way. Which shape belongs where the question mark is?

19

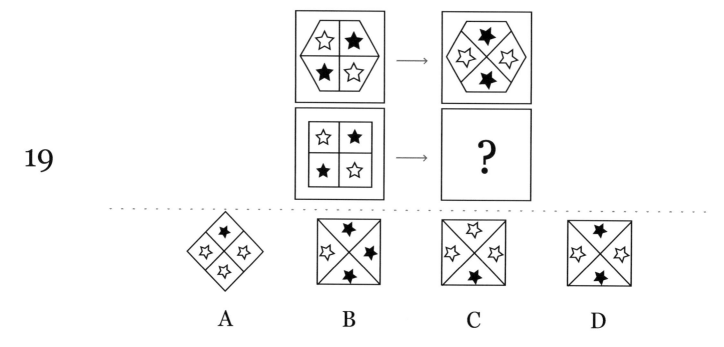

A   B   C   D

Look at the shapes in the boxes on top. These shapes go together in a certain way. Which shape belongs where the question mark is?

20

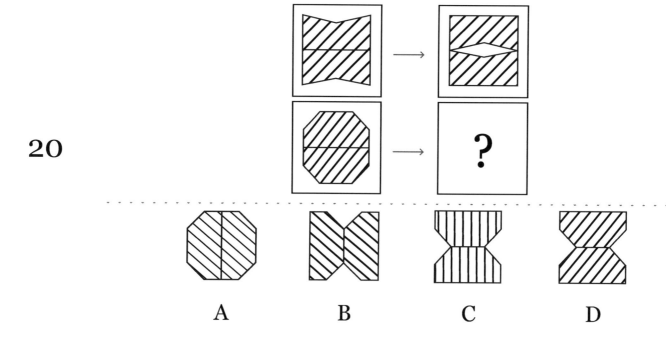

A   B   C   D

QUANTITATIVE BATTERY

• • • • • • • • • •

NUMBER ANALOGIES

• • • • • • • • • • • • • • • • • • •

For each item, the student is presented with two sets of numbers.

The student needs to find the relationship between the numbers in the first set and between the numbers in the second set. Then the student needs to choose a number from the answer choices which follows the same pattern when paired with the number in the third set.

NUMBER ANALOGIES

1. [2 → 4]   [1 → 2]   [0 → ?]

    A. 2   **B.** 5   **C.** 0   **D.** 4   **E.** 1

2. [10 → 9]   [6 → 5]   [12 → ?]

    A. 11   **B.** 1   **C.** 10   **D.** 5   **E.** 13

3. [21 → 10]   [31 → 20]   [41 → ?]

    A. 20   **B.** 30   **C.** 52   **D.** 14   **E.** 40

4. [8 → 2]   [12 → 3]   [16 → ?]

    A. 3   **B.** 4   **C.** 8   **D.** 12   **E.** 16

5. [10 → 2]   [20 → 4]   [30 → ?]

    A. 3   **B.** 7   **C.** 6   **D.** 4   **E.** 10

NUMBER ANALOGIES

6. [**16** → **33**]   [**21** → **38**]   [**33** → **?**]

    A. 33   **B.** 60   **C.** 50   **D.** 38   **E.** 51

7. [**11** → **18**]   [**1** → **8**]   [**9** → **?**]

    A. 54   **B.** 15   **C.** 7   **D.** 16   **E.** 12

8. [**6** → **60**]   [**60** → **600**]   [**600** → **?**]

    A. 10   **B.** 6   **C.** 60   **D.** 60,000   **E.** 6,000

9. [**3** → **15**]   [**10** → **50**]   [**5** → **?**]

    A. 35   **B.** 60   **C.** 30   **D.** 100   **E.** 25

10. [**6** → **2**]   [**18** → **6**]   [**36** → **?**]

    A. 11   **B.** 4   **C.** 6   **D.** 8   **E.** 12

NUMBER ANALOGIES

11. [45 → 45]   [100 → 100]   [0 → ?]

 A. 100   **B.** 10   **C.** 0   **D.** 50   **E.** 45

12. [1/4 → 1/2]   [1/2 → 1]   [1 → ?]

 A. 2   **B.** ½   **C.** 2 ½   **D.** 10   **E.** 11 ½

13. [1,027 → 2]   [4,136 → 3]   [2,641 → ?]

 A. 1   **B.** 0   **C.** 4   **D.** 6   **E.** 2

14. [20 → 10]   [12 → 6]   [16 → ?]

 A. 8   **B.** 10   **C.** 9   **D.** 1   **E.** 7

15. [3 → 9]   [6 → 18]   [9 → ?]

 A. 9   **B.** 36   **C.** 3   **D.** 18   **E.** 27

NUMBER ANALOGIES

16.   [16   →   12]   [18   →   14]   [20   →   ?]

     A. 18   **B.** 14   **C.** 13   **D.** 16   **E.** 24

17.   [16   →   8]   [12   →   6]   [8   →   ?]

     A. 9   **B.** 3   **C.** 2   **D.** 12   **E.** 4

18.   [102   →   1]   [6,114   →   1]   [69,491   →   ?]

     A. 4   **B.** 3   **C.** 0   **D.** 2   **E.** 1

COGAT SCREENING FORM
ANSWER EXPLANATIONS

Verbal Analogies

1. **D.** A candle is made of wax as a window is made of glass.

2. **B.** A dog belongs to the class of vertebrates 'mammal' as a frog belongs to the class of vertebrates called "amphibians".

3. **D.** Football is played in a 'field' as tennis is played on a 'court'.

4. **B.** Cotton is a type of fabric as gold is a type of metal.

5. **E.** Sand makes up a desert habitat as water makes up a lake habitat.

6. **E.** An oar is used to steer a rowboat as a steering wheel is used to steer a car.

7. **B.** Ladybugs have spots on their bodies as tigers have stripes on their bodies.

8. **C.** 'Rein' and 'rain' are homophones like 'there' and 'their' are homophones.

9. **A.** A clock tells time as a ruler measures distance.

10. **B.** A teacher is responsible for students as doctors are responsible for patients.

11. **C.** A triangle has three sides as an octagon has eight sides.

12. **C.** 'Pear' and 'pair' are homophones as 'hare' and 'hair' are homophones.

13. **C.** Nail polish is an accessory that is worn on nails as earrings are accessories that are worn on ears.

14. **A.** The contraction 'I'm' is composed of the words 'I am' as the contraction 'you're' is composed of the words 'you are.'

15. **E.** An immature bee is a larva as an immature fly is a maggot.

16. **C.** A spider builds a web as a wasp builds a nest.

17. **C.** 'Hilarious' describes a greater degree of 'amusing' as 'devastating' describes a greater degree of 'sad'.

18. **B.** A ring is an accessory worn around a finger as a tie is an accessory worn around the neck.

19. **D.** Leopards can be described as 'swift' as snails can be described as 'slow'.

20. **A.** A comb is a tool that is used on hair like a hammer is a tool that is used on nails.

21. **E.** 'White' and 'black' are opposites like 'before' and 'after' are opposites.

22. **D.** A mansion is an extra large house and a shack is an extra small house like a yacht is an extra large boat and a dinghy is an extra small boat.

Figure Matrices

1. **D.** Moving from left to right, the outer shape becomes the inner shape. In addition, the number of sides of the outer shape in the right hand box are reduced by one side compared to the left hand box.

2. **D.** The outer shape stays the same. Inner shapes become mirror images.

3. **A.** Shaded areas turn into unshaded areas.

4. **B.** Middle shape gets smaller and goes to bottom. Bottom shape gets smaller and goes to top. Top shape gets larger and goes to middle.

5. **A.** Inner shape and outer shape each add one side.

6. **A.** Flip shape to mirror image. Add same shape to create circle but with shading opposite side.

7. **D.** Turn shape 180 degrees (1/2 turn in a clockwise direction twice).

8. **C.** In the top boxes, moving from left to right, 3 of the shapes (circles) become 1 larger outer shape (circle), which changes color, and 1 inner shape (circle), which remains the same color as original, but is slightly larger than the original).

The other 3 shapes (squares) stay the same color, but are reflected aacross the horizontal axis and are slightly smaller. In the bottom boxes, moving from left to right, 3 of the shapes (triangles) become 1 larger outer shape (triangle), which changes color, and 1 inner shape (triangle), which remains the same color as original, but is slightly larger than the original). The other 3 shapes (rectangles) stay the same color, but are reflected aacross the horizontal axis and are slightly smaller.

9. **D.** Large outer shape changes from 3D to 2D. Inner shape moves to opposite corner (top) and changes color.

10. **B.** Inner shape changes to new shape, and moves from middle positions to outer corner edges (top left, bottom right). Diagonal stripes move in a different direction.

11. **B.** Number of shapes doubles. Shapes change colors.

12. **D.** Two large shapes flip to create new shape and change color. Smaller shapes on outside of larger shapes flip and change color.

13. **D.** Middle shape becomes 2 shapes and moves to the top and bottom (same color as original). Top and bottom shape become 1 middle shape (same color as original).

14. **A.** Outer shape and arrow turn 1/4 turn clockwise.

15. **B.** Shapes merge and rotate 180 degrees.

16. **B.** Shape flips 180 degrees and inside shapes change color.

17. **B.** Left box on left is a 'close up' of the patterned side of the 3-D box on the right.

18. **A.** Turns counterclockwise 1/4 turn. The black shape at end of arrow changes to white. Two arrows move so arrows are stepped in relation to each other.

19. **D.** The exterior shape stays the same. Interior lines and shapes move counter clockwise 45 degrees.

20. **D.** Top half goes to bottom. Bottom half goes to top.

Number Analogies

1. **C.** Multiply by 2

2. **A.** Subtract 1

3. **B.** Subtract 11

4. **B.** Divide by 4

5. **C.** Divide by 5

6. **C.** Add 17

7. **D.** Add 7

8. **E.** Multiply by 10

9. **E.** Multiply by 5

10. **E.** Divide by 3

11. **C.** Equal to

12. **A.** Double or Multiply by 2

13. **C.** Place Value: tens place

14. **A.** Half Of or Divide by 2

15. **E.** Multiply by 3

16. **D.** Subtract 4

17. **E.** Divide by 2

18. **A.** Place value: hundreds place

CogAT® Bubble Sheet

Use a No. 2 Pencil
Fill in bubble completely.

Name:_____ Date:_____

1. Ⓐ Ⓑ Ⓒ Ⓓ Ⓔ	1. Ⓐ Ⓑ Ⓒ Ⓓ Ⓔ	1. Ⓐ Ⓑ Ⓒ Ⓓ Ⓔ
2. Ⓐ Ⓑ Ⓒ Ⓓ Ⓔ	2. Ⓐ Ⓑ Ⓒ Ⓓ Ⓔ	2. Ⓐ Ⓑ Ⓒ Ⓓ Ⓔ
3. Ⓐ Ⓑ Ⓒ Ⓓ Ⓔ	3. Ⓐ Ⓑ Ⓒ Ⓓ Ⓔ	3. Ⓐ Ⓑ Ⓒ Ⓓ Ⓔ
4. Ⓐ Ⓑ Ⓒ Ⓓ Ⓔ	4. Ⓐ Ⓑ Ⓒ Ⓓ Ⓔ	4. Ⓐ Ⓑ Ⓒ Ⓓ Ⓔ
5. Ⓐ Ⓑ Ⓒ Ⓓ Ⓔ	5. Ⓐ Ⓑ Ⓒ Ⓓ Ⓔ	5. Ⓐ Ⓑ Ⓒ Ⓓ Ⓔ
6. Ⓐ Ⓑ Ⓒ Ⓓ Ⓔ	6. Ⓐ Ⓑ Ⓒ Ⓓ Ⓔ	6. Ⓐ Ⓑ Ⓒ Ⓓ Ⓔ
7. Ⓐ Ⓑ Ⓒ Ⓓ Ⓔ	7. Ⓐ Ⓑ Ⓒ Ⓓ Ⓔ	7. Ⓐ Ⓑ Ⓒ Ⓓ Ⓔ
8. Ⓐ Ⓑ Ⓒ Ⓓ Ⓔ	8. Ⓐ Ⓑ Ⓒ Ⓓ Ⓔ	8. Ⓐ Ⓑ Ⓒ Ⓓ Ⓔ
9. Ⓐ Ⓑ Ⓒ Ⓓ Ⓔ	9. Ⓐ Ⓑ Ⓒ Ⓓ Ⓔ	9. Ⓐ Ⓑ Ⓒ Ⓓ Ⓔ
10. Ⓐ Ⓑ Ⓒ Ⓓ Ⓔ	10. Ⓐ Ⓑ Ⓒ Ⓓ Ⓔ	10. Ⓐ Ⓑ Ⓒ Ⓓ Ⓔ
11. Ⓐ Ⓑ Ⓒ Ⓓ Ⓔ	11. Ⓐ Ⓑ Ⓒ Ⓓ Ⓔ	11. Ⓐ Ⓑ Ⓒ Ⓓ Ⓔ
12. Ⓐ Ⓑ Ⓒ Ⓓ Ⓔ	12. Ⓐ Ⓑ Ⓒ Ⓓ Ⓔ	12. Ⓐ Ⓑ Ⓒ Ⓓ Ⓔ
13. Ⓐ Ⓑ Ⓒ Ⓓ Ⓔ	13. Ⓐ Ⓑ Ⓒ Ⓓ Ⓔ	13. Ⓐ Ⓑ Ⓒ Ⓓ Ⓔ
14. Ⓐ Ⓑ Ⓒ Ⓓ Ⓔ	14. Ⓐ Ⓑ Ⓒ Ⓓ Ⓔ	14. Ⓐ Ⓑ Ⓒ Ⓓ Ⓔ
15. Ⓐ Ⓑ Ⓒ Ⓓ Ⓔ	15. Ⓐ Ⓑ Ⓒ Ⓓ Ⓔ	15. Ⓐ Ⓑ Ⓒ Ⓓ Ⓔ
16. Ⓐ Ⓑ Ⓒ Ⓓ Ⓔ	16. Ⓐ Ⓑ Ⓒ Ⓓ Ⓔ	16. Ⓐ Ⓑ Ⓒ Ⓓ Ⓔ
17. Ⓐ Ⓑ Ⓒ Ⓓ Ⓔ	17. Ⓐ Ⓑ Ⓒ Ⓓ Ⓔ	17. Ⓐ Ⓑ Ⓒ Ⓓ Ⓔ
18. Ⓐ Ⓑ Ⓒ Ⓓ Ⓔ	18. Ⓐ Ⓑ Ⓒ Ⓓ Ⓔ	18. Ⓐ Ⓑ Ⓒ Ⓓ Ⓔ
19. Ⓐ Ⓑ Ⓒ Ⓓ Ⓔ	19. Ⓐ Ⓑ Ⓒ Ⓓ Ⓔ	
20. Ⓐ Ⓑ Ⓒ Ⓓ Ⓔ	20. Ⓐ Ⓑ Ⓒ Ⓓ Ⓔ	
21. Ⓐ Ⓑ Ⓒ Ⓓ Ⓔ		
22. Ⓐ Ⓑ Ⓒ Ⓓ Ⓔ		

BONUS

DOWNLOAD QUANTITATIVE CHALLENGE QUESTIONS

If you also want additional analogies challenge questions, please go to the following link to download them!

To get your challenge questions today, please visit:
https://originstutoring.lpages.co/cogat3analogiesquestions/

Challenge questions can help a student get used to doing the most difficult questions on the test.

Get the questions now at
https://originstutoring.lpages.co/cogat3analogiesquestions

Made in the USA
Lexington, KY
23 July 2019